# Going Through Phases

Going Through Phases
Copyright © 2017 by Alisia Latoi
All rights reserved.

This is a work of fiction. Names, characters, places and incidents either are the product of the authors' imagination or are used fictitiously, and any resemblance to any actual persons, living or dead, events, or locales is entirely coincidental.

No part of this book may be reproduced or transmitted in any form or by any means, electronic or mechanical, including photocopying, recording, or by any information storage and retrieval system, without permission in writing from the copyright owner.

Published by GoPublish, and imprint of Visual Adjectives, Delray Beach, Florida.

GoPublish
14280 Military Trail, #7501
Delray Beach, Florida 33482

Web: www.GoPublishYourBook.com
Email: info@GoPublishYourBook.com

ISBN-13: 978-1-941901-32-8

Paperback Edition July 2017

I'd like to dedicate this book to my family, friends, and youth pastor who have encouraged me to continue to stir up this gift that I have been blessed with.

I'd like to give a special thanks to both my cousin and my sister who continue to be my listening ear and supportive mouth piece.

I love you both.

# Going Through Phases

 by Alisia Latoi

# Table of Contents

## AGE 9 - 14 .............................................................. 8
Alone .................................................................. 10
They Say ............................................................... 12
Voices ................................................................. 14
You Cry ................................................................ 16
I Feel ................................................................. 18
Beauty ................................................................. 20
Lost ................................................................... 22
Get Over It ............................................................ 24
Found .................................................................. 26
Friendship ............................................................. 28
Outcast ................................................................ 30
People Are Just Dogs ................................................... 32
All Equal .............................................................. 34
Queen To Me ............................................................ 36
I AM ................................................................... 38
Someday ................................................................ 40
The King ............................................................... 42
Forever ................................................................ 44
Man of my Dreams ....................................................... 46
Lonely ................................................................. 48

## AGE 15 - 22 ............................................................ 50
Mighty Man ............................................................. 52
Woman of Great Virtue .................................................. 54
Mother ................................................................. 56
Eyes of Wisdom ......................................................... 58
She's Gone ............................................................. 64
Saying ................................................................. 68
Smile .................................................................. 72
Promise Generation ..................................................... 76
Promise to Performance ................................................. 80
9-1-1 .................................................................. 84
Much More He Shall Restore ............................................. 88
Striving, I Shall Be ................................................... 92
Dreams Turned to Ashes ................................................. 94
Doubt, No .............................................................. 96
A Simple Gift .......................................................... 98
Free Mind .............................................................. 100
Once Again ............................................................. 104
Frustration ............................................................ 106
Hi and Goodbye ......................................................... 108
The Overlooked ......................................................... 110
Close My Eyes .......................................................... 112

People in Church .................................................. 114
Still Listening ...................................................... 118
Voice Mail ......................................................... 122

**AGE 23 - 32** ..................................................... 124
Life Still Will Be ................................................... 126
Disappointment .................................................. 128
Apologize ......................................................... 130
Risk ................................................................ 132
Admission ........................................................ 134
Rejection .......................................................... 136
Never Loved At All ............................................... 138
Original ........................................................... 140
Silent Expression ................................................. 142
If I Change ........................................................ 144
Memories ......................................................... 146
Daydream ......................................................... 148
Can't Help It ...................................................... 152
It's Time ........................................................... 154
Window ........................................................... 156
Rocking Chair .................................................... 158
Fault ............................................................... 160
Count Time ....................................................... 162
Colorful Paper .................................................... 164
I Went ............................................................. 166
Hesitation ......................................................... 168
Romance Me ..................................................... 170
Can I Talk To You? ............................................... 172
Skin Tight Jeans .................................................. 174
I Don't Feel The Same ........................................... 176
Friend ............................................................. 178
Tug ................................................................ 180
Infinity ............................................................ 182
Dreadlocks ....................................................... 186
I See ............................................................... 190
My Strength ...................................................... 192
Thirteen ........................................................... 196
U-Turn ............................................................ 198
You Drink You Sleep ............................................. 200
Closet Eater ....................................................... 204
Purity Shoes ...................................................... 208
Swallow ........................................................... 210
Counting Pennies ................................................ 212
Paper Plates ...................................................... 218

# Age 9 – 14

# Going Through Phases

It began at the age of nine. I was being innocently mischievous. My dad yelled and gave me his famous stern look that my siblings and most of my cousins have feared and have now grown to respect. I ran to my room in tears and retaliated the safest way I knew how. I grabbed a pen and paper, then wrote.

Eyes just staring at me
Wonder what it's thinking
Wonder why it does that
I can't stand it any more
It's just staring at me
It scares me
With those devilish eyes
Look like they're turning red
Why is it staring at me?
Why?

And I kept writing. This method of expression became the arms that hugged me when the touch from humans felt unnatural.

# Alone

# Going Through Phases

Sometimes I feel like

I'm all alone wishing for

Another way home

# They Say

# Going Through Phases

They say things that hurt me

So much

I can't describe

Hurts so much

Feels so bad

Why won't they stop

I wish I knew

And when they say these things

I sit there and reply

I am who I am and

I'm proud of who I am

# Voices

# Going Through Phases

I hear voices in my head

One's bad and one's good

It's hard for me to decided which one to listen to

I get so frustrated

I just want to scream

Which one should I listen to

It's hard for me to tell

Which one is bad

Which one is good

I wish they would just stop

# You Cry

# Going Through Phases

People say you shouldn't cry over nothing at all

They say that everybody has problems and you should just get over it

But everyone will cry at some point in life even if it's over nothing at all

Even if you have a good life with no problems

You still have to cry sometimes

Just to let out frustration and sadness

You cry

Or to let out pain and happiness

You cry

They even say that boys shouldn't cry

Crying is for girls

But even boys cry sometimes

It's not that you're weak or your acting like a baby

It's just that you're human

Humans cry

# Going Through Phases

I feel all alone
I feel like nobodies home
I feel like an egg just waiting to crack out of its shell
I feel so scared
I feel like I'm in a homeless shelter
I don't know what will happen next
Am I going to live or
Am I going to die

# Beauty

# Going Through Phases

What is beauty?

Beauty to me is found within

Everyone is beautiful

In there own way

If God made you

He makes nobody ugly

Beauty

Everyone has it

Before you judge someone else

Look at yourself

Does everyone around you

Think you're beautiful

But frankly

It doesn't matter what other people think

God made you beautiful

Not only on the outside

But on the inside too

# Lost

# Going Through Phases

Lost inside a dark place
Never to be seen
Can't run
Can't hide
Can't move
Can't go anywhere
Can't do anything
Don't know what to do
But continue to sleep
I wake up to another place
An empty place
It looks like something is missing
So I walk
To a place full of anger
It makes me feel locked inside
Then I crawl
To a good place
It feels like Heaven
I wish I could stay here
But then I'll see another day
And go through each place again
For once I wish I could be free

# Going Through Phases

Every time I pray
I wonder if He's listening
Every time somebody lets me down
I wonder if He's hurting
Why do I always seem sad
Why do I feel so mad

Get over it

Every time I lose a friend
I lose a part of me
Every time I get in front of a crowd
I feel like they're all laughing at me
Why do I feel so empty inside
Why can't I just find a friend
Why can't I just be happy
And

Get over it

Sometimes I get jealous of my sister
When I'm by myself, I cry
But I wonder if any one hears me
Why do I feel so low
Why am I always so sad
Why do I get so mad
Why can't I just be happy
Oh why
Why do I feel

# Going Through Phases

Lost inside myself

With the world surrounding me

Wondering through the misery


I step upon a place

With amazing grace

Not even knowing where I was

I went inside just because


I was down and

I haven't been found

I needed to be loved from

Somebody up above


When I was there, I went

Off in a cheer

Because my life is undone

And now I'm going to have fun

# Going Through Phases

Friendship

Talking, listening

Calling, helping, goes out

Happy, longing, sad, excited

communication

# Outcast

# Going Through Phases

An outcast

Treated like an alien

But human

Feel like a human

Act like a human

Don't think like a human

Looking at the moon and the stars

Wishing I were in Heaven

Wanting and aching for the holy touch

Wishing I could see His majesty and the embrace

But I'm hear on Earth

Waiting to find out my purpose

Crying sometimes

Wishing I were dead and in Heaven

Right now

I don't care how I die

I just want to be in Heaven

Alisia Latoi

# People Are Just Dogs

# Going Through Phases

People are dogs.

You never know what they

Are thinking

Dogs can act mean or nice

So can people

Sometimes dogs will bark at you

Just the same, people will

Sometimes yell at you

People are unpredictable,

So are dogs

People are just plan dogs

# All Equal

# Going Through Phases

This earth God created

Has many things

That are in it

And those things that are in it

Are too many for one to name

Some are big, some are small

Some are bad, some are good

But we were all created

All by one

All created equal

Just like one

We are all different

In many ways

But still equal

Just the same

# Queen To Me

# Going Through Phases

She's so special indeed
She gives you what you need
And although she can be very mean
She's still the all time queen

Even when she's down
She'll give you the crown
She'll love you all around
Because that's the sound of a mother's song

She'll do her best
To beat the rest
She gives you a nest

How could it be
To have a mother so free
Who loves all of me

Sometimes I'm sad or mad
But then I see my mom
It makes me glad

I know she loves me
Even though she doesn't tell me
She shows me
She'll always be a queen to me

# Going Through Phases

I am a Christian girl who loves Jesus

I wonder what it looks like up in Heaven

I hear the cries of the people who get killed every minute of everyday

I see the Angels up above helping people from below

I want to live in a peaceful place and not worry about getting hurt

I am a Christian girl who loves Jesus


I pretend that I am an Angel praising the Lord everyday

I feel loved by the one who created me

I touch the untouchable

I worry about my family

I cry when I see other people cry

I am a Christian girl who loves Jesus


I understand that God is forgiving

I believe that there is a limit to His forgiveness

I dream of a peaceful place with no violence or evil

I try to do right in God's eyes

I hope that someday I will make it in to Heaven

I am a Christian girl who loves Jesus

# Going Through Phases

I hope someday my
All time favorite wishes
And dreams will come true
That someday I will find the
Man and the friend of my reflection

# The King

# Going Through Phases

He's lean and mean
He's the household king

He'll give you the best
Sometimes less

He'll work in the dirt
And deal with some jerks
When you're telling lies
He'll give you those eyes

He'll be the strength
Of his child's life

He's the boss
He'll never get lost

He's the first creation
Of God's new nation

Even when he gets old
And ends up being a heavy load

He'll still be lean and mean
Tall and strong
The world's all time king

# Going Through Phases

I love you

And I know you're always with me

There are time when I feel differently

I wish I could touch you

I wish I could see your face

Always

I wish I could hold you

I wish I could stay in your arms

Forever

If only I could touch you

If only I could see your loving face

If only I could hold you in my arms

And stay there

Forever

# Man Of My Dreams

# Going Through Phases

The man of my dreams has to love me for who I am

He has to love me no matter what I look like

He will be sweet and charming

Nice and kind

Tall and handsome

White or black

He will be strong and a believer of God

The man of my dreams has to be perfect

But of course

Nobody's perfect

# Lonely

# Going Through Phases

I can't seem to explain the emotions
I have no one around me
Should I call this a gift
It's no fun being lonely
Why should I put a smile on my face
When the only person around me is my shadow
I hear no sounds
No voices
Just the thoughts that cloud my mind
I am tired
But there is no rest because my desires never seem to be fulfilled
Even among people I am still left by myself
My heart stands alone
I'm past empty
The hopeful light of God
My eyes barely see
What is next
Blindness
Until I fade away to complete nothingness
Will someone help me
Rescue me
I'm lonely

# Going Through Phases

I grew up in church. My mom brought my little sister and I there religiously. Bible study and Sunday services were shows that we were not absent from as a child. I'd look forward to the days my mom would dress me in the finest attire her pockets could afford, just to see the pastor put on his cape and lay hands on someone who would then magically fall to the ground. It was all entertaining. My childhood eyes thought I was witnessing superman in action.

By the time of my youth, church became my hope for a cure. I thought myself to be wounded and church my healer. Through out my teenage years, sermons consumed my every thought and influenced my every action. I felt unaccepted, needed someplace to run too, and put all of my hope in a building full of dressed up people with cloudy hearts.

# Mighty Man

# Going Through Phases

O' mighty man of valor
I have a job for you to do
Just don't be blue
I have called you by name
No need to be ashamed
You are not lame
Although you may be feeling pain

O' mighty man of valor
Do come forth
Don't limit your worth
You where brought with a price
Stop rolling that dice
Your chances are slime
Vision might be dime
But I am the ultimate gem

O' mighty man of valor
Can't you see
All that I want you to be
I chose you above the rest
Out of them you are the best
Although you will have to go through many test
I want you to be my guest
Have some fresh wine
As we dine
No need to stand in line

O mighty man of valor
Don't be deceived
Although you can't perceive
The blessing you are going to receive
Don't ever leave
Because with me you can achieve

Just believe

# Going Through Phases

I am a virtuous woman
Not to be disrespected
I am a virtuous woman
Not to be neglected
For centuries you've tried
To kill this woman inside
But in His arms I lie
I will not die
You've tried to beat me
Until there was no me
You've tried to rape me
But there was no taming me
You've tried to silence me
Until there was an uproar of violence in me
You can't contain me
A woman of great virtue
Can't be controlled
How interesting I am
From all the rest
Continue to administer your test
I am pure and holy
Tried and true
You just have no clue
How precious I am in God's sight
You can't have a bite of the treasure
That lies within
I am saved only for the man who is to be my twin
Who will secure this pearl
Not to be called a slut or a tramp
This is a virtuous woman
Not to be disrespected
This is a woman of great virtue
Not to be neglected

# Going Through Phases

What does my mother need
On what does she feed
I cry to you O' God
On my mother's behalf
All day she toiled
In the sun her skin boiled
Father, I know my mother wailed
And Father, I know sometimes she has failed
In the evening I prayed and saw my mother's tears
God, you know, it brought me fears
Because my mother is everything to me
She is the reason why I am on bended knee
Father, I know I owe her a fee
Because those tears were for me
I don't deserve her
But Father, you bore her
You've open every door for her
Spoken that her life has just begun
She has yet to see the morning sun
Under cover, you've trained her to be a queen
Only in her daughter's eyes does her royal procession lead
Her birth pains didn't end when she saw my life begin
Her pains continued until
I saw the Son
I'll eventually know what a mother endures
But I now know that her love cures
This is a daughter's cry
For all her mother's beauty to out shine the sky
I want her to know that she is adored
I want her prosperity to out run the door
May her finances be blessed by the Lord
And may her riches be more than she can afford

# Eyes of Wisdom

# Going Through Phases

Looking through eyes of wisdom;
Age and time has made her;
The deepness of the sea,
Connects her to me,
The sun sets and rises
As she opens her eyes to see that God still has a purpose for her
To rise to the surface;
The song she sings will never change,
The love she gave,
Shows me that she's brave,
She's not afraid,
God is her aid,
As she lays in the pillar of fire,
She realizes the devil is a liar,
She sees things that I can't,
Knows things beyond my years,
Knowledge that I long to hear,
Her thoughts are that of God,
Her discernment beyond my comprehension,
Humble is she,
Has no choice but to be
Strong and gentle at the same time;
Equally balance,
Amazing to me,
Bore so many children,
Yet still strong,
Fought so many battles,
And still walking on,
Her soul is at peace,
Her prayer is complete,
She is at liberty,

The devil is under her feet.

# The Women of His Heart

# Going Through Phases

I'm watching Jesus being crucified
The woman who touch the hem of his garment
He healed me from the issue of blood
And now I see His blood pouring down
I wonder if I should stand strong
I can't bear to see my lord suffering
So I bow my head and cry because
I fear we're losing our king
I know His time is ending and all I can think about is if I'm worthy

Am I worthy enough for you to die for me?
Nails in your arms and legs
You're shedding your blood on Calvary
Am I clean enough for you to stay on that cross?
Would you forgive my sins because without you I'm lost
Am I worthy

How is it, just moments before this I was anointing your feet with oil
My tears washed, as my hair dried
Never have I felt so honored
Am I in the presence of my savior?
Hung on a cross called pain
Every ounce of me wishes the cross was mine
Am I the reason you're being crucified

Is there a way for me to stop this?
I thought that I would never see the day that all would accuse you of something you would never do
But as I see your blood pouring down and your skin ripped from its bones
All I can do is worship you


I worship you, even while you're on the cross
I still feel your holiness, even though your flesh is torn
Lord you're worthy
With thorns as a crown, I still see your royalty
I love your majesty
My forever worship


My son
I watched you come out of my womb
Now I witness you dieing before me
The flesh born from my own whipped and tossed aside
They're striking him so many times
Until all you can see are the bones on his back
By what strength does he survive this long?
The sounds of his painful cries torment my soul
I think back to his childhood
He called for his mother and I went to him
Now he's on the cross

# Going Through Phases

He's calling for his father but I don't see him
What I do see is his blood dropping as they beat him
I clean the red off the ground
Why did God choose me to bear this king?
What should I do?
Can I rescue you?
Do you remember when I picked you up from the sand?
Raced you to the house and let you win
Do you recall all the talks we had?
When I made you laugh
And you heard me sing
When the angel told me of this gift named Jesus
Elation filled me
Today there is fear
I never knew that I'd be watching you die
Look at me my son, see me, and watch me cry

God, you selected me, so I must be strong
He is a king and he must take his throne
He is a king but he still remains my son
He is a king and he must fulfill his calling
He is a king and I will be a part of his following

# She's Gone

# Going Through Phases

Every time I see you cry

It's like a thousand tears

And every time I see you smile

It's like a million fears lifted

You've crossed many oceans and your sky is clear

Rest assure, you've raised me right

And I still have many years

So, mama, why you sitting with your head down low?

God's placed a crown on your head

When I look into your soul I still see a child

So go a head and hug your Heavenly Father

He's been waiting on you for quite a while

And when I look into your heart

I see you've ran many miles

But go a head and cross the finish line

You've won your race for sometime

Mama, don't worry and don't give up

You could have all rest in the mist of your storms

As you pray and as you sleep

It is I who ask God for eternal peace

Can you see the crown on your head

Don't you know that it is my life you have guided


I wish I had another chance to say that I love you

I wish I had another opportunity to reach my arms out and hug you

So many moments I took for granted

I thought that I would always see your presence

But now you're gone and you're giving God His holy reverence

Now I'm standing all alone without a mother to be my guidance

When I think back to the time she was here

I ask God for forgiveness for all the times I was disrespectful

I wish those memories would disappear

If they did, would I still be the same woman


I wonder if I was ever the cause of your tears

I wonder how many of your prayers were for me

Did you know that I once dreamed of you in an all white robe

Adorning a crown shinning in pure gold

If I had to choose

I'd be the angel whose only job is to protect you

Mama, If you could see through my eyes

# Going Through Phases

Then all the diamonds that surround you are true
On heaven and earth, you are royalty
Your rich quality has hopefully been passed on to me
While you were here and now that you've gone
Your beauty is what I share

# Saying

# Going Through Phases

"Keep your head up"

Is so easy to say

Saying, "Things will get better"

Won't take the pain away

If I say, "Hold on, be strong"

Would you trust in me?

If I say, "The storm won't last long"

Would you have faith and believe?

The smile on my face will brighten your day.

Hopefully it has the power to take the aches of life away.

You tell me,

"One storm goes and another one comes.

It never seems to end.

I get a break in between and then it starts all over again.

I remember when my mentality was to take life as it comes, but

Now I wish my life would pause so that I could prepare for the next storm."

Then I say,

"Through your silence I see that your hope is fading.

The expression on your face reveals that there are a thousand words formulating.

Not every storm deserves your precious thoughts.

Some storms cause no damage.

Some obstacles produce no spots."

Then I say,

"Words of encouragement won't help, unless you let it.

Life won't let you down, unless you expect it.

Without faith, you might as well count life lost.

Dear friend, God always reveals His light.

If I'm wrong then everything I know about life will be proven false."

# Going Through Phases

# Going Through Phases

Don't lose your smile

It mirror's my reflection

Don't lose your smile

It's my sun when my sky is cloudy

And when the rain starts to fall

On both sides of the world

Don't lose your smile

It seems as though life is hardest on you

Where some walk to obtain

You have to run to get through

It's easy for me to say that there's sun in the mist of rain

But my sister, in all honesty

Where there's pain

There's more pain

There is never one rain drop

But there are millions within a minute

However, it's never everlasting

The sun will show its face

You'll see it

The rain feeds the plants
But the sun causes them to grow
You can't develop in life unless your joy shows

Don't lose your smile
It feeds your soul, increases your strength, and makes you whole
Don't lose your smile
It'll be all worth it in the end
One day you'll look back and say
Even when I struggled
My smile showed signs of victory
Even in the mist of struggle
My smile showed me that the sun will reveal its face again
Love finds itself in you
It's the love you have for yourself that sees you through
Although you have fallen
You will rise
Although you have been bruised
You are not broken
Although you have cried

# Going Through Phases

You will rejoice again

My sister,

When your path seems cloudy and your vision unclear

Don't lose your smile

Because a rainbow is drawing near

# Promise Generation

# Going Through Phases

Who are the youth of this age

People who have no need to live in a cage

Leaving all for the sake of the call

Yet still they fall

I am appalled by the youth that call themselves generation-X

But I am not afraid

Because there are youth that call themselves Generation Next

A generation of promise

These youth are ablaze for Christ with His flame they will fight

The promise generation will worship and pray all night

We are youth that pant after God

As the deer pants after the waters

So our souls pant after thee

When the youth of God speak

All demons must flee

Because we are the head and not the tail

We will never fail

We are above and not beneath

Nothing shall be taken from us by a thief

We are royal priesthood

A holy nation

Laying prostrate before God is our station

Worshiping Jesus in spirit and in truth

Is our dedication

We are youth that are on fire

And because of that God is constantly taking us higher

He is multiplying us a thousand times more

Just watch

He is opening every door

The devil has lost

We've carried our cross

And now it's time to wear our crowns

Nothing shall hold us down

We are the chosen youth and the only thing we stand for

Is the truth

# Going Through Phases

# Promise to Performance

# Going Through Phases

The wind will continue to blow

The sun will continue to shine

The moon will set its glow

And the rain will fall in line

Waves shall roar

Eagles shall shore

The earth shall sake from its inner core

Even the universe shall adore

The stars will sing

The planets shall bring

Praises to the King

Let us sing

On whose hand they hang

Whose fingers shape the clouds

In thunder they shout out loud

Because of His power

Even the demons are bowed

The lion shall not bite

The bear will not fight

At His name they will stop on sight

With His might

You can shine your light

He promise to give you all power through His name

In this we proclaim

In this He called our holy frame

To now perform what He has ordained

With faith the size of a mustard seed

You can move mountains

With one thought

He'll give you the knowledge to subdue giants

At your request He will part the sea

Just utter His name

And all demons will flee

It is time for us to perform

As of now

You have been warned

If you can't do what God has put inside of you to do

Then you have no clue

# Going Through Phases

You're still questioning whom

When He has said

It's you

So get off the promise

It has been dismissed

It is time to perform

What God has ordained

# Going Through Phases

9-1-1 no more time for fun
You can't even see the shining sun
Everything is left undone

Can the remnant of God stand
Will the remnant of God take their land

Planes collide
Buildings slide
People died
The remnant of God abide

Are you the remnant of God
That is my question
I am the remnant of God
That is my confession
What is the remnant of God
That is my life's lesson

9-1-1 emergency
People of God
Where is your urgency?

Alisia Latoi

God has left but a few
To enter in the mourning dew
And to walk refreshed and anew

God will save the leftovers
And Satan, He will discover

9-1-1 the people cried
As bodies lied
The remnant of God did not hide

The remaining is sustaining
Not fainting
But attaining and gaining
Hope that is raining

Only the remnant take God's hand
And enter into the Holy Land
In the end the remnant will stand

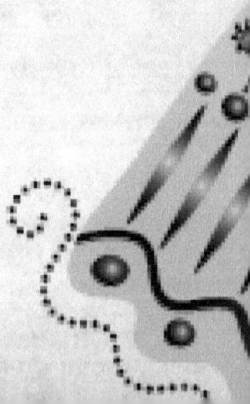

# Going Through Phases

# Going Through Phases

He's existing in the trees

He's existing in the waters

Where ever we are

He's existing in us

When we fall into deep despair

We turn on the songs of Zion

His spirit begins to minister to us

Though it seems like the devil maybe winning

Trouble around every corner

We still have the victory

Nothing can happen to us that God hasn't already predestined

No road block can stop us from getting to were God would have us be

His will shall be done

I shall not worry

The same God that got me through before, shall get me through again

The same God that took me out of a deep cave

Shall not leave me in another one

The hope that I put in the Lord shall recover me

His presence will rest upon me

I now have light in the mist of the darkness

I now have peace in the mist of the storm

I now have joy in the mist of sadness

This joy doesn't have to bring me a smile

This joy calms my soul

What rejoicing I shall feel when I see the Lord's face

When the evil of this world ceases

In His presence I shall have peace

Drawing close to Him as He draws close to me

The thought that He takes joy out of spending time with me

This sack of filthy rags

His blood washes me white as snow

If he can transform the night into day

How much more can He transform me

Just to look more like Christ Jesus

That's where I want to be

If He can, with His mighty hand, save a house from being destroyed from a tornado

How much more will He save me from the hands of the enemy

If He can provide food for an ant

How much more will He provide for me

If He can watch over the flowers of the ground

# Going Through Phases

How much more will He watch over me

Much more is the key

He shall do much more for me

Destroy this temple and He shall resurrect it

Break this body and He shall restore it

I mean that much to Him

Through all tribulation

He shall do more

He shall restore

He shall bring peace

All evil shall cease

No more crying

No chance of dying

You could say goodbye to all falsehood

In that place

We shall finally see His face

With His amazing grace

Living with His holy race

Feeling His great embrace

You can erase all the traumas and trials

God will replace them with smiles

# Striving, I Shall Be

# Going Through Phases

As far as the distance in space

Do you seem to me

But as close as the clothes on my back

Are you

As tribulation and persecution are all around me

I know that I am more than a conqueror

Though the vision may seem so far and despair so near

Complete joy seems to be only a dream

Heaven as the air, which I will never see

I know that above exist a God, my father, who is and is to come

He is the reason I have peace in the mist of the dark clouds

He is the reason why I can place a smile on my face and be hurting inside

When life seems as meaningless as trying to look for the end of a rainbow

Hoping to find gold

I know my treasure is in Heaven

My goal is to get there

Every step I take to get higher and closer to Him

May be slippery and I might fall

But it only inspires me to keep going

My father in Heaven knows

He knows my hurt, tears, and sorrow

He knows that right now the pain seems to last forever

Just around the corner is a man who will consume me with happiness and peace

I'm striving to please Him

In His hand lies my wholeness and fulfillment

In His hand I shall be

# Going Through Phases

The gold at the end of a rainbow
The shooting star that the child wishes upon
Hopes placed on the candles of a birthday cake
It all stops

The light burns away
The gold doesn't exist
The shooting star, no longer seen
Dreams turned to ashes
Hope fades away
Aspirations and desires that drive you through life
Slowly disappears as the way seems more dark
As you walk this dead-end path
The zeal for life drowned
Visions fail to become a success

Who can rekindle this life of desire
The light of God will take existence higher
Filling hope with fire
Without God, dreams turn into ashes
Aspirations and desires dependent on God will not fail
Through a long trial
There will be no failure

# Doubt, No

# Going Through Phases

My heart is broken

And I haven't even spoken

I've shed so many tears

And I haven't grown in years

Why do I bear so much pain on the inside

And carry so much weight on the out

Why does it seem like my prayers just fall to the ground

And my visions just keep tumbling down

How can I keep a smile on my face

When I'm looking for a warm embrace

And how can I keep my head up when everything around me is pushing it down

My faith is telling me to keep on going and that my vision shall live on

But how do I know when the Lord is going to show

My uncertainty is sure

This I know

But I'm waiting for the Lord's answer

This is how I know He'll show

Because He won't leave me in a pool of uncertainty

No, He won't let this be

You won't let your sheep walk on unsteady ground

You said you'd always be around

# A Simple Gift

# Going Through Phases

I ran out of money

What can I say?

But I couldn't see you without giving you something on Christmas day

Not only do I celebrate the birth of Jesus

I also celebrate all you're worth

More than all the riches in the deep blue sea

The love of God is the only thing that's free

In you are treasures that can not be denied

When we gather together as a family that's where God abides

I'm happy to see you

May God saturate you with His mourning due

Until we meet again

Stay with God and you'll always win

This is my simple gift

My words can't be measured by every width

I hope this means more to you than a present brought from a store

I love you

And I pray that God opens every door.

# Going Through Phases

Did you hear that?

Wait a minute, I'm the only one here, so who am I talking to.

And who's talking to me?

So many voices in my head

I have to be free

I hate my parents

I hate me

Killing myself is an option

Wait a minute.

What am I saying?

Who is in my mind, giving me these thoughts?

If I don't stop, I'm going to hurt someone or me.

I have to be free.

Who is talking to me?

Insecurities are trying to take over my mind.

I'm so ugly.

No, wait, I'm just fine.

God has given me beauty not ashes.

I have to be free.

It's so dark in here.

Evil spirits cause me fear.

Frighten by the voices inside,

So scared, I have to run and hide

So that I could be.

I have to break free.

I can't take this anymore.

To much going on in my life

No time for peace

Only time for strife

I can't live on this earth anymore

It hurts too much

So many voices in my head.

I'm so confused.

Too many tears I shed.

I have to be free.

O' God, set me free.

Whom the Son sets free is free indeed.

It is your words I read

# Going Through Phases

In order to break this bondage

I have to succeed.

Fly.

Sour.

The sky is mine.

Am I finally free?

I shall see.

# Once Again

# Going Through Phases

For some reason, I keep falling in the same area of my life.

I've been taught that God is merciful and willing to forgive.

But what if I keep asking for forgiveness of the same sins?

Are you willing to forgive me?

Will you have mercy on me?

I am a repetitive soul, who never seems to learn.

When approached by the same obstacles, I fail to succeed conquering,

I end up on my knees, repeating the same overused prayer,

That has, in my mind, become haunting.

Will you forgive me once again?

For I have fallen to the same sin.

How will I lift my head up high, if I have one weakness, one of whom I can't say goodbye?

The pleasure felt good for a moment.

Until my thoughts lead me to repent.

A feeling of guilt and shame has caused my head and knees to once again be bent

And repeat the same overused prayer.

Are you willing to forgive me once again?

For I have fallen to the same sin.

# Frustration

# Going Through Phases

My thoughts surround me
Why should I compare myself to everyone else
Why should I base my life on the opinions of others
Just because they say I'm scared
Does it make the word true
Just because they say I'm not good at something that I do
Does it make the opinion real
My life only belongs to me
What people say fill me with negativity
So I have to encourage myself
Is that so hard
Yes

My purpose isn't clear
Come to think of it
I'm consumed with fear
Because I don't know why I'm here
I see my vision for a moment and then it becomes unclear
I would follow the footprints in the sand
But they washed away last year

There is no chaos in the universe
The stars know when to shine
Sun knows when to set
Where is the order in my life
Where is my God who will end all strife
Will he bring peace to my night
I'm frustrated

# Going Through Phases

Look into my eyes
And see the color of my skies
Then you'll know the reason why I can't fly
And you'll know the reason why all I say is hi and goodbye

I am down
Because I have nobody
I smile
Just to set my heart free
When I'm bound
Chains hold back my victory
Life causes me to fall at times
Because dark clouds crowd my way
Somehow I still keep the faith
Because I know there's a holy place
And I end up on my knees
God why isn't life heavenly

Yet still I cry
Can't see a brighter day
When night falls the stars are my only guide
Lord when are you going to answer my constant prayer
Without ears that listen
Conversations are pointless
So I just say hi and goodbye

# The Overlooked

# Going Through Phases

I use to be someone you couldn't talk to

Now look at me all opened and bruised

Who will ever know me

There is too much going on inside that no one sees

If you look into the eyes of a human soul

You'll see more pain than laughter

And that is what has the world torn

How is it that the most beautiful people on this earth are left alone

And the hardest soul has the world sold

People are quick to run to those who are cold

And the warm hearted are left in a corner

Getting ready to cross an empty road

The best people in life may not have many friends to hold

They look in the mirror and are sad because it's like they're worthless gold

Are you like me

The overlooked and the passed by

The underestimated, closed up, and the forever cry

The so called shy, quiet, and the perceived loner to whom no one says hi

Then like me

You hear a voice that says one day we'll meet in the sky

In one fire there are many flames but the cause of it is all the same

Every person may turn away but there is one who still remains

He knows you in every picture frame

Alisia Latoi

# Close My Eyes

# Going Through Phases

Can I be

What I see in me

What once was motivating is disappearing

Do I still sleep and dream

Do I still pray and believe

Should I speak positively or just face reality

My strength is gone

My faith has been worn and torn

How do I keep on going

How do I push my storm

I envision greatness

But can I really obtain it

If God puts a vision before my eyes

Does that mean the path is mine

If my future isn't eminent in my lifetime

Then God please stop teasing me

Take my dreams

Take my hopes

Close my eyes

# People In Church

# Going Through Phases

Tell me why do the people in church make it so hard to be saved

They tell me to come as I am, but once I come, they want me to change

They tell me I act too wild

Pull down your skirt and you're showing too much cleavage

God gifted me with this size, it's not like I can get rid of it

Your pants are too tight and butt too big

Well, if their were a surgery to reduce it, would you provide me the funds

You dress too sexy

Who are you trying to impress

No one but God so why don't you give it a rest


Tell me why do the people in church make it so hard to be saved

When I raise my hands

They say it's not high enough

When I shout

They say it's not loud enough

They sit there in their same old church chair

Telling you to join the choir

Get involved

Yet when you do

They critique and say don't get big headed

This ministry is not about you at all

Tell me why do the people in church make it so hard to be saved

They speak in to your life as though they are God

Saying you have an evil spirit

You better get your life right

You're having too much fun in church

This is a holy temple, not your backyard

How are you going to listen to worldly music and then give glory to God

Calling me the hypocrite

Yet I love all without judgment

# Going Through Phases

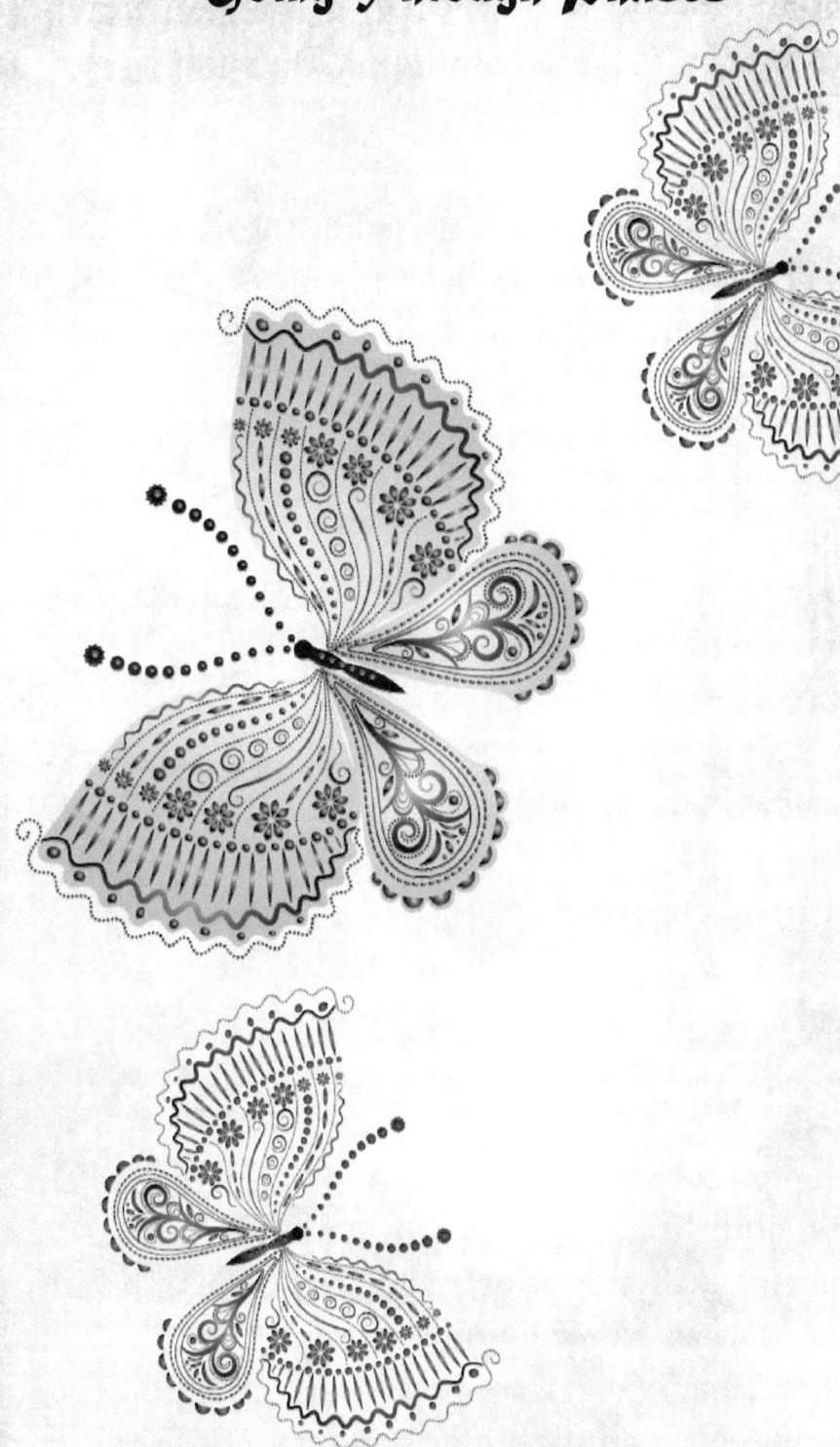

Alisia Latoi

# Still Listening

# Going Through Phases

Does God really love me because life just won't keep still

When I cry, are you there to wipe my weeping eye

How can I fly with wings of eagles if there is a lighten bolt in every storm

Where is my life you promised abundantly

Would you still love me if I needed some clarity

Life brings swift changes and gives no time for my spirit to heal

If happiness is healthy then why isn't it all I know

If I don't rejoice through all things

Did I sin

If I complain through the hardship instead of giving thanks

Did I lose and not win

If I doubt my purpose because I can't find direction to reach my goal

Will heaven be a place for my eternal soul

Sometimes I wonder if you are real on this earth

Because the grave, I can touch

But your appearance, I don't see much

Who can look directly at the sun and still have vision

Who can see everything that goes on spiritually and still keep there sanity

Right foot, show me the way

Left foot, stay focus today

Body, don't let me down

I'm trying to see if my Father is around

God, you must know that I feel your rays of light

My hope lives on despite the knight

I use to hear your voice whispering

When I was younger, you where holding me

Now that I am older, you get quiet at times

But I want you to know that your little girl is still listening

# Going Through Phases

# Voice Mail

# Going Through Phases

Restore to me the joy of my salvation
Restore to me the joy of your love
Cleanse my heart and make me whole
I want to experience the glory of your presence
Let me feel you
Touch your garment
Be familiar with all of your ways
I bow down and worship your holy name
Renew my mind
Father
Draw me near
I want to know you
and be rid of all fears

Even though you're seated in heavenly places
Will you come and talk to me
Trouble's around every where I turn
I look up to find some relief
God, please pick up the phone
It seems like every time I call
Your line is busy
I leave a message and get no reply
If you could simply step off you're throne for a second
I need to hear your voice
The world is getting worse
And life is getting hard
I'm trying to stay saved
But I'm not getting far

# Going Through Phases

By the time I got a taste of independence, I felt as though I had heard every sermon, and saw every two toned face that I could see. I left; not my faith, but I left a building, a business, and people no better than those outside. I went, I found other topics, and fell in love with life.

# Going Through Phases

I could hold on to what hinders my joy

I could ponder all night the words I didn't say

I could let them fall

since

Tears are healing to the unrelaxed soul

or

I could keep alive what should be dead feelings

Darkening my heart

While life still goes on

# Disappointment

# Going Through Phases

Failed expectations

Cause disappointment and regret

Both feelings suck

I'd rather be disappointed with myself

Climbing my own ladder to redemption

I hate to be letdown by someone else I esteem

If I minimize my expectations in others and in the universe

Will I find less disappointment


Is it possible to erase all hope in mankind

I feel the urge to

Destroy this wall in which I lean

Close my ears to the footsteps that lead and follow

Change the color of the air I breathe

Relying on no one to achieve

Presidency over this soul

Whose faults I know, love, and evade

# Apologize

# Going Through Phases

Why won't you apologize

If you know you've hurt me

You're too blind to see your selfish pride

And humble yourself by saying, sorry

Then you look at me as though I'm something funny

As if I'm discovered mold, that's rotten and ugly

Why don't you clean and wash me away

Like dirt that falls before your eyes

Forgiveness is foreign where you lie

And because of this your skies are forever dry

# Risk

# Going Through Phases

Should I cut my hair
And pair it with an outfit
I wouldn't normally wear
What if I approach this guy
Fall in love
Then three years down the line
Because of him my heart and anger collide
If I play the lottery with my life
Everyday each decision brings
A consequence I can't see
If I stay where I am at
I may face the same misery
But if I go someplace new
The face of a darker path
May show
Down each road
There could be a blessing or a curse
The fear of the unknown
Belittles the excitement of new challenges shown
What if I lie awake all night
Trying to figure out my next move
Will it be a waste of time
If in the end, no matter what
My fate is to lose
If tomorrow has already decided itself
Can my worry and indecisiveness fade away
Just let the waves carry me
Allow my mind to find peace
My body to sleep
And trust tomorrow's brighter day

# Admission

# Going Through Phases

I'm scared
Can I admit that
And sometimes
I confess to my journal
The times I really just don't feel attractive

# Rejection

# Going Through Phases

It took a lot for me to approach you

Confess my affection

I thought maybe after dinner and conversation

Interest would spark

It's not easy for me to walk up to you

Say hi

Reveal my heart

So if you would be so kind

If your feelings are not in line with mine

Then turn me down gently

Please reject me while showing signs of sensitivity

# Never Loved At All

# Going Through Phases

I've seen couples walking hand in hand

And I've seen the look in a woman's eyes as they gaze at their husband

I see them around town

Sitting together as if their is no one else around

They have a glow of happiness

A light that I have yet experience

It seems that I can only watch as two lovers kiss

That is one touch I have never had

And therefore, miss

I long for a man to hold

Love is wonderful

At least that's what I'm told

I think that love is running away from me

If it is before me then I just can't see

I simply pray that one day

I will feel its company

# Original

# Going Through Phases

An original is full of misspellings,
Misunderstandings, scratch offs,
And rephrases

# Silent Expression

# Going Through Phases

Writing was my get away
My secret, silent expression
Sending me to a place that holds no judgment, malice, or deceit
My sadness, joy, anger, and frustration was once only shared with my pen and paper
My tears were evident through letters
Sealed tightly between the arms of the invisible
I lost my secret place

For a while, I could not find my words
My thoughts became void of direction
Years passed without a documented lesson
The days I tried to embrace my beloved pen and paper
My thoughts offered me silence
Emotions over took me due to my hearts rejection
I have no release
I thought I'd simply forget what I once loved
Not possible

Writing is my hiding place
It liberates me
My beloved is my home
I've missed him
Without expression
My body has a deformed soul
A letter journey called me by name
This pen, paper, and I are the same
I must resuscitate the red beat of my heart

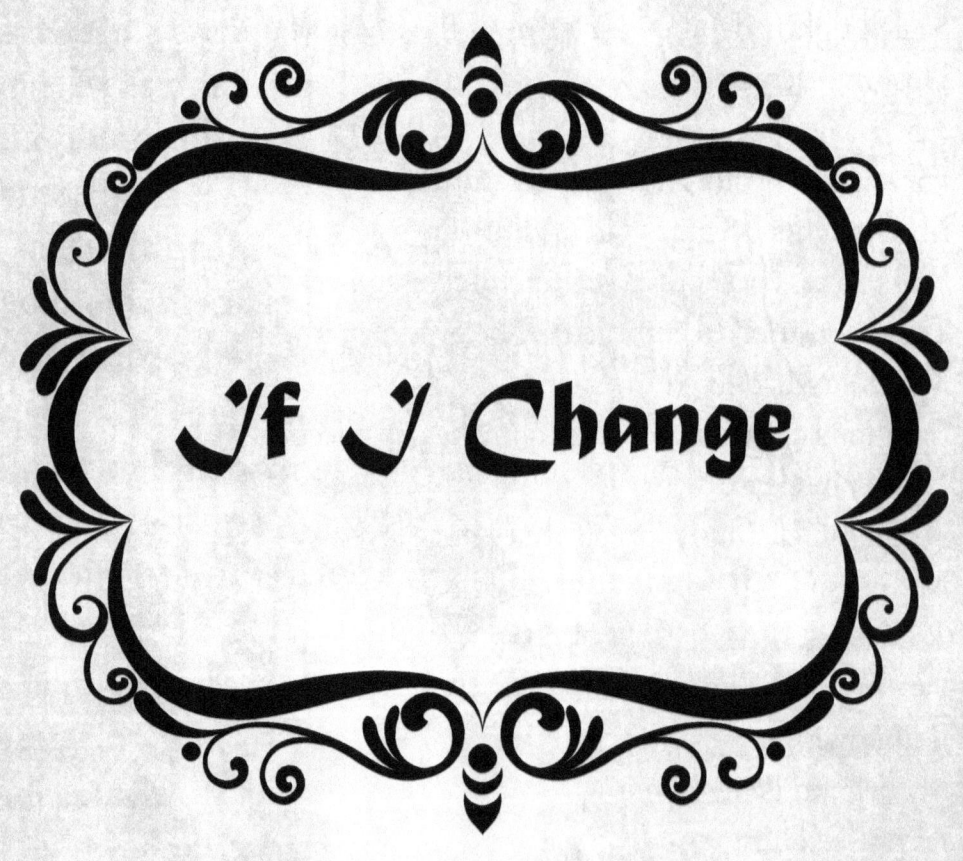

# If I Change

# Going Through Phases

Twenty five years old
And I'm still questioning me
Is there something wrong with wanting what use to be
Life changes
Brand new faces
Empty places
Heart expresses
So I'm different
An innocent bystander
A little bit quiet
And this scares the stranger
I'm not that easy to get to know
It's almost impossible to get my feelings to show
I've spent my life trying to change
Change the way I walk
The way I dress
Be more talkative
Outgoing
Open up
The effort was frustrating
I just wanted to be loved for being me
I thought that if I changed
Then maybe my circle of friends would grow
If I changed
Then maybe I'll feel more accepted among my family
If I changed
Then maybe the guy I wanted would finally look at me and stay
But what bird can say
I don't want my wings
What dog can say
I don't want my eyes to see
I'm twenty five and realize
I need to learn to accept that I am
Who I'm meant to be

# Going Through Phases

I don't expect you to help me move on,
But your friendship may help me one day
Be okay with the memories.

# Daydream

# Going Through Phases

In my daydream

I am pretty happy

Just play pretend

No reality to make me sin

There's no hard thinking

What's my plan

Everything going my way

This is my land

Can I stay in this daydream

Do I have to ever leave

No one's here to condemn me of this evil deed

I just stare somewhere

There's my man

He looks at me in my fantasy

As though I'm his lover and best friend

I see him

In actuality he doesn't see me

But in my daydream

I'm all he needs

He holds me and kisses me

Who knows if this will ever really be

All I know is that I'm smiling and it feels good

If I ever decide to look around
Then I'll know that all I'm really looking at is wood
So I just stare
If time passes by
I don't even care
He's beautiful
But am I to him
Only in my fantasy
I'm bigger than most
In which, I don't like to boast
But in my daydream
I'm so lean
His arms can fit around me
So happy I'm not poor
I have money stored away
A place to stay and a car
This is only my far away star
There is no war
No one to cry for
Until I wake
I'd rather dream
I don't want to feel reality anymore

# Going Through Phases

# Going Through Phases

I can't jump to conclusions

I can't be expectant

My heart can't avoid being broken

Even still, I keep my defenses up

If I observe and don't experience the pains of life

Will my journey still have meaning

I hold back my love

Because I don't want to hurt

But I can't help to hope

That you're the one I deserve

# It's Time

# Going Through Phases

Time to renew my smile
It's not worth a frown
Time to straighten my walk
I refuse to fall
Time to make things right between you and I
Time to learn to talk
I don't know why we fought
Time to come together and share one last name
Time to declare our love
I"m not playing
No more games, it's time we start living
No more pain, the rain is gone, and I'm done giving
No more teasing, it's over now, cause I'm not pleased
Get with me, it's time you get down on bended knee
I gave you four years of my life
Where is the ring
I want you to call me your wife
Do you love me enough to be real
Can you tell me how you feel and be honest
I want you to be my love but if we can't get it right then I'm done
No more games, I love you, and I'm not playing
No more pain, time to get with me, and end the bachelor life
No more teasing, you've got the ring, and you're on bended knee
Get with me, he said
I'll marry you
Cause this is meant to be

# Widow

# Going Through Phases

Fate never skips a day
Destines are tied effortlessly
Their love endured a long ride
The sunset forgot time
The hardest part will be dealing with the memories
Because before him there was no reality
Years of his touch couldn't be duplicated
Store bought cologne without the frame that wore it
And what will she do with all his clothes,
Donate it or store it
Time becomes so valuable when the secrecy of death is exposed
A cancer eating the flesh
One day there's the excitement of planning a wedding
Today there's the dread of standing alone
Forty years
Now you're a widow
Who would've fathom you walking down this path so soon?
Forty years
Now you're a widow
The tears didn't fall until she touched her husband's gloom
Lifeless body, expensively suited, and staying in a hole
Now this widow is faced with what is to her truly unknown.
The hope of Heaven brings a smile to her face
The reflections of a rare love
One could only wish to experience such grace
As the choir song, "I'm going up yonder to be with my Lord"
The images of dancing lights might someday be concrete,
If this widow can't stand to be by herself in this earthly place.

# Rocking Chair

# Going Through Phases

She sits by the window with wondering eyes
She has a song in her heart and a golden disguise
Her body is torn because age doesn't heal
She's not revealing the pain that she feels
But she knows in her soul that it won't be too long
Til' Jesus comes back
Sees her in the rocking chair
And carries her home

Until then she sits around
Swaying her cares away
When I'd see you with a smile
It would take all the people on earth to say
Just what you mean when declaring
Everything is okay
Somehow I know that there are things you've seen and never shared
I know that the deepest tears you've ever shed
The Lord has bared
And I know that when you were on your knees in the middle of the night
God was always there to answer your prayer
As the days went by
While you sat in your rocking chair

# Fault

# Going Through Phases

I,
Me,
My fault,
My problem,
Never we

The situation,
My surroundings,
My life,
My choices,
My regret
Never yours

He's involved,
She's involved,
Your words
Never mine

He confessed,
She confessed,
You made the mistake,
Your choice,
Your wrong
It's never me

You're to blame,
I'm put to shame,
For your actions,
And my reaction,
To a temporary satisfaction

# Count Time

# Going Through Phases

These are the best times

Where innocence is maintained

And laughter is still laughter

Not tainted by regret and pain

Childlike reality and illusion hold a thin line

My son, purity sustains your healthy heart

Imagination transcends time

These are the best times

When Iron Man is just a toy

Not a metaphorical image of your reflection,

When your emotions are not protected behind imitated strength

And cruelty is not retaliated with manufactured violence.

I miss the times

When sexual desires don't overshadow the acts of a common gentleman

The respect for one's parent outweighs the need to belong

Instead of involving yourself in the acts of mischief, you felt the need to come home.

These are the best times

Witnessing your birth and death in my lifetime

The best times become a memory and a question

Was my love worth your time?

# Colorful Paper

# Going Through Phases

Colorful paper under a decorated tree;

Celebrations among dressed up beings;

Shouting, "Because of the birth and sacrifice of Jesus Christ, we have victory."

Families smile in spite of a hard year;

Preaching, "Let us over indulge on sweets and demonstrate some Christmas cheer."

Giving, without the prospect of receiving;

The best colorful paper contains a gift consumed with sincerity.

Unwrap the present of joy from the ones held dear;

Open the prayers of blessing towards the new year.

May the comfort of angelic wings surround your heart;

And continue to fill you with the aspiring radiance

That sets you a part from all the other

Colorful paper under a decorated tree.

# I Went

# Going Through Phases

I spotted you when no one else was approaching

I fell in love with someone who never held my hand

I got crushed by a giant wearing sandals

# Hesitation

# Going Through Phases

I know you're just a man

That I shouldn't place on a pedestal

Before I even got to know

The scars on others' caused by your hand;

You seem beautiful to me

Dressed in the disguise of my glossy eyes;

But I haven't seen your flaws

So I label you perfection

If I could only confess this a lie

Then I could speak to you without hesitation

# Romance Me

# Going Through Phases

Give me a dozen roses
While I show you all my poses
Romance me several times and my heart will find
That your fragrance left my mind in a trance
Light some candles and my attraction is enhanced
Sing me a song and my body will dance
I lose all function just by your one glance
Your thickness has increased
Your true talent has been released
Get with me and I'll throw you a Thanksgiving feast
The table is set come taste my yeast
Take control because you've unleashed my inner beast
Start the fire
I'll feed you chocolate
Take me higher
Look up, it's our rocket
Grab the holy word
While I teach you my bible study
Eyes haven't seen nor ears heard
What will be in our story
Look into my eyes
It's no surprise
That I'm into you
Kiss me until the sunrise
While I write my rhymes to the moon
Touch my shoulders that way
Down to my hips as I sway
Caress me gently while I lay
My heart out to you throughout the day
Feel my curves
Calm my nerves
With your soothing words

And a love song is what we'll both say

# Can I Talk to You?

# Going Through Phases

I usually have so much to say
But for some reason before you my tongue is contained
You have so much power over my body
One look in your eyes and my knees become weak
I lose all mobility
Forget common words
It's no wonder I'm silent
Beseech me, I'm yours
You're difficult to read
Your mind intoxicates me
Intelligent and attractive
A good combination
You must agree
I usually have so much to say
One look in your eyes
With you, I could imagine spending the whole day
Do you not know the power you have over me?
One smile, one touch
And I swear, Heaven has set me free
I see so many possibilities
Long walks, endless talks
My curiosity only intensifies
Every time I learn something new about you
Your frame captivates my eyes
But it's your mind that keeps them glued
I choose you to seek
So wake up drifting thoughts
Mouth, it's time to speak
I usually have so much to say
What electricity
What attraction
Tell me,
Do you feel the same?

# Skin Tight Jeans

# Going Through Phases

I'm not the one wearing the bikini at the beach

I'm not the one in skin tight jeans

Ain't it funny how your eyes won't land on me

Is it because I'm not a petite beauty

I'm just an average girl with a little pudge around her belly

And it's hard getting you to notice me

You may go for the ones with the big boobs, skinny waist, and large derriere

But honey, you need to get with me

Believe it when I tell you

I'm the one who will love you best

There is more depth to me than that girl who has your eyes glued to her skin tight dress

I may not be the model or video vixen

But if you want a girl who is there for you and not just about looks or putting on a show

Then I'm the one you should be getting to know

See I'm an average girl in a masqueraded town

With imperfections that can be seen

I'll never fit in her size two pair of jeans

You'll always see my stretchmarks

With my visibly over-sized heart

# I Don't Feel The Same

# Going Through Phases

You were once all I thought about
Your style, your walk, I craved to see
I drove my friends crazy with every mention of your name
But situations changed and I'm not the same
My heart was once yours, but it isn't anymore
Don't come to me this time
You had your chance
Now the opportunity is gone

We use to sit around and laugh
I adored the way you held me
Excitement painted my face in your presence
The way you couldn't resist not making me smile
Cause you knew I would go wild

You hurt me
I turned and there you were, next to her
You thought you played a fool
When I found out, you couldn't say a word
And when that relationship was over
You came running to my door
I didn't answer
I don't feel the same way anymore

# Friend

# Going Through Phases

I saw the pictures on your profile

You're with some woman that's not me

I have to convince myself that she's not pretty

And that you don't look remotely happy

I sometimes close my eyes and envision you walking towards me

The look in your eyes read that you want me

I immediately watch imaginary images depicting our future

Full of days going out and nights staying in

Excitement sends chills throughout the outer layers of my skin

Then reality sets in

You spoke to me and I spoke to you

We flirted with our smiles

And uttered words unspoken with our eyes

Then our lips touched and that's when I knew that you felt

The same as I do

We floated on waves

I was convinced this was it

I've meant my prince

It was time to confess my all

I wanted to finally give you the boyfriend title

But my perception mislead me

A friend was all you saw

# Going Through Phases

A tug of love
I pull one end
You pull the other
The bind is strong

Until I give more than he offers
The conclusion draws nearer
But I'm not ready to let go
My focus becomes sharper

The rope is long so
I heave a little harder
Will my opposite companion propel
Or move farther

He yanks and I yield
But my grip is more resilient than my shield
I dig my shoes deeper in the mud
Take a firmer stance and tug

Forgetting to exhale
My muscles shake as I drag
And he yells, cruel and forgiving words
While we play this silly game

I look behind me and see more cord
The image in front shows he's moving forward
One last jerk, now I see the hairs on his skin
No distance between us, I win

# Infinity

# Going Through Phases

Out of hundreds, your eyes caught mine.

What was it that first attracted you to me?

Was it my exotic curves, the way my face shined upon the sun's light?

You drew nearer to me.

Admiring my interior features, in awe at the sound of my alluring voice.

Our first few dates were full of surprises.

You introduced me to your family and friends,

Took me to the Keys for weekends,

Spoiled me with the finest up keeps,

Including weekly washes and a full tank of premium gas.

I was your first luxury, the Infinity of your dreams

A sign of accomplishment.

Truly, I loved you and the attention you gave.

Together we drove all hours of the night.

You wooed me with Luther and swayed me with Maxwell.

We went to clubs and parties.

I hated the closely compact parking.

You left drunk that night and foolishly decided to drive

We crashed into an eight wheeler

I was totaled

But you survived.

Alone for days

Towed away like a 98 Corolla.

My engine was rusty but my leather seats were still warm from your touch.

I was anxious for them to repair me so that we could ride once again.

Then I saw you.

I thought that you would be walking, but you drove up with what look like one of my cousins

A BMW, maybe

No, she was of the same make and model

An Infinity with a different shade of gray.

The look on your face told the whole story,

I had been replaced.

# Dreadlocks

# Going Through Phases

If I move in a little closer to you

Touching your hand

Do you feel the same tickle

I do

I don't want to be the first

But I can be a bit impatient

I must know

Do you kiss slow

Is your cream minty

If I glide up your cone

Spend the most time

Making you moist

Will you bend

And wrap your dread

See them

Lock around me


If I tease my pedals

Dressing them with my favorite scent

Will your eyes mirror my gleam

Mine shine

As I look at your frame with curiosity

Do you like to enforce pressure

With steady rhythm

While on top

Will your energy stop at my navel

Or reach the apex of my nipple

If I take you to the edge

Will we feel the vibrations

That will make you worn enough

To release your dread

Witness them

Lock around me

If I paint my colors on you

Stroking every corner

Leaving no marks bare

Will you reflect my image

I'm innocent

But my lips taste guilt

Come in to my water

I want to bath you

# Going Through Phases

With my satin rags

Slowly convert you

If I do

Will you then cast your dread

And

Lock them around me

# Going Through Phases

I see my frailty,
My loss, and inabilities
Some I accept and others
I challenge
Leaving pieces of me
A casualty

# My Strength

# Going Through Phases

Alone I find my greatest joys and darkest hours

While searching for relationships of all kinds

Many have failed

Some succeed

In becoming something long lasting

Still feelings of loneliness creep in

If I forget that the most important relationship is the one I have with myself


Many have called out characteristics that would quickly be denied

At the time, I thought them to be a weakness

Now I acknowledge them as assets


I am emotional sometimes

Even though I try not to be

The tears flow easily

Empathy, sympathy, and on rare occasions self pity

My face leaks

I am sensitive

Only when hearing words from those close

Speak with caution

My reaction can portray self defense or hurt


I am a loner

Not hesitating to retreat to myself during communal events

Finding conversations with strangers uncomfortable

Hiding in a shell is the social fix


I am a quiet person

Getting lost in thought

In the absence of a paper and pen, ideas are forgotten

Reluctance to speak produces a shy smile

But yet

I am bold

In the most unforeseen moments

Concocting a remark that shocks audiences

My reservations leave room for unexpected courage

# Going Through Phases

Infatuated with being an introvert

Never to be considered a weakness

The traits are a great strength

I've discovered and embraced my inner wealth.

# Thirteen

# Going Through Phases

Age thirteen
Arms sag
Stretchmarks defined
Nose wide
Lips sparkle
Fingernails have that purple shine
A fat girl Barbie

Brown skin
Bumpy face
Crocked teeth
Coiled hair
Stood straight
Bent to tie her shoe lace
Chocolate super hero with no cape

Stubby girl
Expanding layers
Square glasses
Clothes with holes
Walks on toes
Scrubbing thighs
While she glides on her vision of golden skies
Thrift store runway model

Head held high
Embracing uniqueness
Smiles while others mock
Tripping over every elevated sidewalk
And still speaking that sassy talk

She is esteemed

# U-Turn

# Going Through Phases

Don't make a U-turn

He may have changed

But there is no need for you to conduct an experiment

Just to see if he has new ways

# Going Through Phases

First step

Admit you have a problem

Dad hasn't ate all day

Because he's slept passed time

His room is filled with empty cans

His life is tied with mine

But he's a stranger just the same

I check for signs of sleep

Just to see if he's still alive

Second step

Change old habits

Every day the same routine

Like clock work

You drink, you sleep

I brought your favorite

Red and white cans for your birthday

You didn't seem to enjoy the gesture

I thought it would've been appreciated

Repeatedly you ask my mom to buy red and white cans

Intoxicated you slur
Babble on, and disrespect her
That virtuous woman, she clings on
Once married, separated, and then back on
Time passes
Dad's fifty now
You drink, you sleep

Third step
Redemption

I remember the summer of no drinks
So vividly my mind escapes
To Disney with the family
You were so energetic
We were so happy
I thought deliverance had come
Then back home, life went on
Red and White cans, the light through your storm
You drink, you sleep
I'm not your savior
So my life must go on

# Going Through Phases

# Closet Eater

# Going Through Phases

Close the door

I can't bare them staring

Exposure is intimidating

I can talk to my friend at any hour, day, or night

My crutches fill me to capacity

Always by my side through full or empty times

I keep them in my closet of secret gluttony

Crunch one, crunch two

Got to be rid of the calories

Come lay on the couch

Confess your telltales

Insert all that you have gathered from the fridge into your mouth

It's the coins tossed into your wishing well

Plates all clear

Throw it out before anyone sees

The only item left in that cold space

Are baby green leaves

Push up one, push up two

Got to be rid of the calories

Clothes still fit

That's great news

The stretchmarks, however, still reveal your past rendezvous's

In hiding when you didn't know how to tell your appetite to stop comforting you

Once down the drain

You felt embarrassed at the witness of your own greed

Jumping jack one, Jumping jack two

Got to be rid of the calories


Time for confessional

I eat behind walls

My portion size no one knows

So that on me, judgment will never fall

I push down my emotions with produce that smell and taste so divine

Swallow them whole

My dirty laundry that no one will ever find

Run ten minutes or until consumption is forgotten

The mirror reveals the truth every time

Keep running

Bury those crutches and your body will fall in line

# Going Through Phases

# Purity Shoes

# Going Through Phases

Isn't this too soon
I may be the only woman my age
Still wearing purity shoes
You had my attention initially enticed
Then you questioned my sexual history
Found there to be none
Your focus stayed on that one topic
Your mission was to hold the gun
Be the first to shoot bullets into my womb
I laid there thinking
Might as well
Who waits til marriage anymore
You said you'd ease it in
But it felt like force
Closing my eyes
1,2,3, breathe
This is how much my purity shoes are worth
I laid there thinking
He doesn't yet know my last name
Do we share common interests
Couldn't we at least do this on a bed
Instead of on a couch at your sister's house
He goes in again
Closing my eyes
4,5,6 breathe
I'm giving my purity shoes away
I laid there thinking
He is attractive
He'll be less of a stranger the next day

# Swallow

# Going Through Phases

As a young girl I observed you
Watching the Heat game
You'd swallow, laugh
Swallow and cheer
Not one conversation between father and daughter all day
You'd swallow, go pee
Swallow and sleep
To the back porch you'd sit
Swallow, stare into nothingness
Swallow and drink more beer
Then you'd meet the line of intoxication
You'd swallow again
Swallow and have the best relationship with your cans

I'm here at the bar, all grown up
I pay attention
As I swallow, laugh
Swallow and cheer
Have conversations with friends and meet new strangers
Continue to swallow, laugh
Swallow and cheer
Head to the club
My night is not finished
I swallow, dance
Swallow and drink more vodka mixed with cranberry
I hate beer
It knows my father too well
Caused him a DUI and an overnight stay in a jail cell
I decide to end my night
Way before the point of intoxication
Stop swallowing and head home

Before he becomes my reflection

# Counting Pennies

# Going Through Phases

Coin 1989

My mom took my sister and I for a ride

She said my daughters, I'm leaving tonight

But I promise everything will be alright

I'll be staying in a one bedroom apartment

But you'll still see me before every moon

Just know that your dad and I are separating

Things will no longer be as you are use to

Then she stopped at a near by store

And said pick which ever candy you would like

I caught her pulling out the brown paper roll of coins to pay

And then I realized she was counting pennies

And things may never be the same


Coin 1995

Saturday morning

Mom bust into my room

She said lets go shopping for clothes

School is starting soon

I jumped up

Alisia Latoi

I wanted to enter middle school with the best clothes

My mom pulled up to K-Mart

And my disappointment showed

Three bottoms, five tops

Not the latest fashion

Two pairs of shows from Payless

One black, one white

That will go with every outfit

You'll still need to wear last years closet items

This is all your parents can afford

She looked into the eyes of my sister and I

Providing hope

I'm counting pennies right now

Maybe next year will be better

Maybe then

I'll let you pick the store


Coin 2001

It's senior year

There are lots of activities

# Going Through Phases

Class trips, senior breakfast, graduation photos

A class ring and a prom dress that shows my curves

As I sat and went over this list with my parents

They resounded

That all seems like fun

How much will it cost

What about college, I asked

Your dad and I are separated at the moment

Financial Aid should help you pay

But here are some pennies

This is all we have saved


Coin 2007

I'm sitting in the drive way

My parents are back together again

But I'm not living at home

I thought I'd adult it

Try living on my own

My heart is anxious

Thinking about the conversation from last night

When I spoke to my mom

Told her my car is on the verge of repossession and I might be evicted

If I don't get financially right

Can you loan me some money

Come over, she replied

Now here I am

Embarrassingly, standing at the door of my childhood

Mom left me alone to discuss the issue with my dad

The one person I was attempting to avoid

The one man I secretly try to impress

Water fell down my face

When I told myself not to confess

That I'm counting pennies

I'll step on my pride and ask you

Father

Help


Coin 2012

I can still hear my sister cheering

# Going Through Phases

Reminiscing at the moment I received my college degree

It took me twice as long as the average person

But I finished

Today I walk through the doors, to a job, not a career

You're still living coin by coin, I see

I am too

My mom mentioned on the phone during my lunch break

Your dad and I are separated for real this time

We may get a divorce but it's expensive

All in all, I'm alright

How are things on your end, she asked

I replied

I'm about to start paying for an education that cost twice as much

As I make in a year

I'm one month behind on every bill

Right now, I'm in between paychecks and at a machine

Counting my pennies

Trying to walk this tight rope called life

But other than that

I'm doing just fine

Alisia Latoi

# Paper Plates

# Going Through Phases

My sister and I, as kids we use to slide

Down the hills after the rain

Using our endless supply of paper plates

Whoever reached the bottom first

Would take ownership over the big brown box

Our pretend castle

We use to flock to our favorite tree

Every Saturday morning

To see who could imagine the best story

Using our toys that cost little to no money

Until dinner time when mom would beckon us to come inside

Help gather the food

Bring it to the dining room

She'd always request

Then all would sit waiting to eat

While mom fixed dads plate made of ceramic

She would remind her girls

The head of the household never uses plastic

Now my sister and I are at a coffee shop

Down the street from our childhood story

Every Sunday we'd meet to discuss current happenings

Today, I proceed to tell her my tale of the week

You know how I've been giving online dating a try

I've meant men here and there

But this one guy was a contender

We'd go out and camp in my small brown box apartment

The attraction was evident

He'd call and text with little delay

Showing the most potential

Then one day he mentioned seeking only the disposable

Being blind to relationships long- term

I immediately gave him paper plates

So that he could slide straight out the door

I paused to gaze at my sister

Remember when we would imagine

ways to use toys that cost little to no money

We would equate the waste to riches

# Going Through Phases

Looking back, it's funny

How perfect the disposable was for our time of innocence

Now I want nothing to do with plastic

That day, my sister and I took an old walk back to our favorite tree

Reminiscing on the box that was a huge part of our history.

Follow Alisia Latoi on Social Media.

FACEBOOK: "Books by Alisia Latoi"

www.Facebook.com/alisialatoi/

INSTAGRAM: @Alisia_Latoi

Alisia Latoi can also be reached via email:

alisialatoi@gmail.com.

# Author's Bio

Born and raised in South Florida, Alisia Latoi received a Bachelor's in English and Sociology at Florida Atlantic University.

Writing poetry since the age of nine, her poetry style is free form and Alisia's first collection features poems written in her early years, adolescents, and young adulthood.

www.ingramcontent.com/pod-product-compliance
Lightning Source LLC
Chambersburg PA
CBHW021145080526
44588CB00008B/217